ENDS OF THE EARTH

ENDS OF THE
EARTH

KATE PARTRIDGE

University of Alaska Press, Fairbanks

Text © 2017 University of Alaska Press

Published by
University of Alaska Press
P.O. Box 756240
Fairbanks, AK 99775-6240

Cover and interior design by Kristina Kachele Design, llc.
Cover image from *Antique Sea Creatures & Monsters* Collection by Catherine Haugland,
theavalonrose.com.

Library of Congress Cataloging in Publication Data
Names: Partridge, Kate, author.
Title: Ends of the earth : poems / Kate Partridge.
Description: Fairbanks : University of Alaska Press, 2017. | Series: The
Alaska literary series |
Identifiers: LCCN 2016056625 (print) | LCCN 2017013264 (ebook) |
ISBN 9781602233331 (ebook) | ISBN 9781602233324 (paperback)
Subjects: LCSH: AlaskaPoetry. | BISAC: POETRY / American / General.
Classification: LCC PS3616.A7847 (ebook) | LCC PS3616.A7847 A6 2017 (print) |
DDC 811/.6DC23
LC record available at https://lccn.loc.gov/2016056625

CONTENTS

*

It is a profound, vexatious, never-explicable matter—this of names.
I have been exercised deeply about it my whole life.
—Walt Whitman, "Specimen Days"

ENDS OF THE EARTH

When Siduri saw Gilgamesh coming up the road,
she locked the door and went to the roof:

her inn, despite his protests. Imagine:
she's washing the cups, setting them

one by one in the wooden rack; pots cleaned
for that day, at least; gulls shredding

the last scrap of meat from the stew
tossed in the yard. Tonight, a glass of wine

by the fire, by the shore, perhaps; perhaps
with a guest, but ideally alone, humming

some melody she can't label as minor,
but dark as vinegar, or desire.

*

My old GPS doesn't work in Alaska, so I've reverted to paper maps, which I
love: their soft rustle, the requirement that you have at least a general sense of
geography before using them.

I spend a great deal of time nodding along while people tell me about driving
to X or Y, then run home to look up which side of the state that's even on.

What's fortunate: most places are reached by one road, if any at all.

*

Donne writes in "Hymn to God, My God, In My Sickness" of his movement toward death in cartographic terms:

doctors become mappers, body
        strait and passage, owned, named, inhabited. In this metaphor,
     the body cases insight, the future:
   my west.

*

Great liberties have been taken in constructing Alaska to one's own specifications—my favorite, a map printed in 1593 in Antwerp within a collection of speculative charts. I suppose the inaccuracy is part of the charm, as in a child's grasp of botanical fact in a drawing of daffodils. Alaska was not even spotted by Europeans until 1741, when a Danish explorer left eastern Siberia and saw it by accident.

*

Gilgamesh said: *Tavern keeper*

when you saw me
why did you bar your door
    and
mount the roof terrace?

I will strike   *down your door;*
I will shatter   *your doorbolt.*

He's looking for the underworld, and its signs.

*

In Alaska, unfamiliarity often seems undercut
with a little danger. For instance, I meet Lydia
on the Chester Creek Trail in August,
when she emerges from a bank of fireweed

carrying two fistfuls of mushrooms and offers me one.
I don't eat it—I've just read this Robert Hass poem
in which he picks a bad mushroom—but she extols
their value for cooking and tells me all about

moving from Russia anyway. She next reappears in March
by the lake, her pink windbreaker suit now swapped
for a blooming purple, waving some plant with wild gestures
at a man in hiking boots who clearly wants to get away.

*

The Antwerp mapmaker had some fun with names—he marked the top
half of the landmass Anian Regnum: anticipation of the Northwest Passage,
using a title from Marco Polo (who had no idea where it was, either).

The lower half: Quivira—moving target of Coronado's search, a North
American city of gold. A mask for error—if the gold isn't in Kansas, it must
be in the one place we haven't yet touched.

*

Alyse and I walk the trail along the mudflats—
post dinner, post drinks at Darwin's,
the sun tucks down at eleven.

The inlet ice has begun to shift
in plates—lips jutting underneath,
pressure lofting the chunks over

magnificent clods easily mistaken for rock.
At the end of the world, mountains
form a barrier against invasion, she says.

*

In his grief, Gilgamesh lets his hair grow out and dresses in furs. I let my hair
lengthen, too, but for a much less glamorous reason: it's cold.

In what is either a compulsive or a thrifty act, I use the same five bobby pins
every day during the awkward phase, tucking them into a pocket when out of
use, fingering them lightly on walks.

*

On early maps, boundaries are sites of inquiry rather than edges,
consistently shifting and fantastical: the potential
                    for something else
greater or more awesome than.

Mount St. Elias, the smaller brother, soon taller than Denali.

*

The mapmaker's sea is occupied
by a unicorn-mermaid creature, not particularly ambitious

about the ships approaching her from all sides.
The ships, not so competent in their roles, either—

one is firing its cannons to the opposite side
of the monster. It seems the kind of creature capable

of afflicting the coast with apocalyptic acts,
the kind that require a hero like Gilgamesh

to rescue the land—not quite Four Horsemen,
but still great in her destructive reach.

*

Some Alaskan grocery stores carry big barrels of dehydrated food products. One is simply labeled "breakfast"; the image on the front indicates that eggs, bacon, and toast may all be contained therein. The signs above the displays say things like "preparation" or "emergency," although I often wonder if they just mean "alarmist."

*

J. wants to practice at the range with his bear gun
before he leads summer hikes in the Wrangells,
but every time he goes to buy ammo, the day's lot
has been purchased by the old men who line up
before opening to stock bullets along with barrels
of food in their bunkers. "All over town," he sighs.

*

What shall my west hurt me? As west and east
In all flat maps (and I am one) are one,
So death doth touch the resurrection.

Is this the land of riches, swift passage—
or the end of the road?

*

I meet a man who lives off the grid and gives me directions to his home using the mountains and a creek. I have a general sense of the location, which I suppose is his goal—if I went up there and yelled, I would find him, but that's as close as I could get on my own.

I have chosen an apartment at 22nd and A.

*

When the scorpion advised him to travel
through the mountain, the darkness was so great
that Gilgamesh could not look back.

Siduri said, we have drink, food, music,
hot bathwater, death.

Reverse:

Life, which you look for, you will never find.

MODEL

As if the name isn't enough,
she insists that I stand on the porch, too,

to look at the beaver moon,
which is indeed pale as the rings

around birches along the river, or bright
enough to light them, and barely obscured

by the early evening streetlights and sirens,
the icicles grafting onto each other

in regimented curtains. Here
and there, one takes an abrupt turn

where it's been dripped on—
sudden elbow tapering out.

My friend says nothing can be done
about the icy intersections except patience,

but he also recommends wrapping
a turkey in bacon, so take your best guess.

The term *fishtailing* makes me wonder
what it would be like to be propelled

by sudden shifts from behind or to wade
across a street completely submerged

in fins. The ice seems suddenly preferable.
In fact, we snap off ice spears

from the roof and compete, perhaps
not as safely as one might, at hurling them

into a snowbank, where they remain
wrapped in snow as though modeling

the rule for treating impalements:
leave the object in place.

AFTERSHOCK

Even in the moment, I'm disinclined to think
my end will be this: watching the kitchen

shelves shed themselves while I sit cross-legged
under a chrome-rimmed table, a relic older

than this oil-age apartment dispatching
its contents in the quake. It's still dark, morning

when we've parsed glass from the rug, righted
the shelves sprawled on the floor, extracted

medicine bottled in the sink. In some organized
street tracked by tires, a pulsing plow may be tossing

a thick birdseed of salt to the ground to draw
us out. The ravens may have taken their place

on the electric lines along 15th. It may still be
that our boots would puncture the thin lip of ice

on snow like a tin window ornament pressed
from behind—but there remain no guarantees

in the cold. It may or may not be the day frost
gathers in my eyebrows, or the day the postal worker

leaves another nudging note to shovel better,
or the day the air leaps back from my lungs

in a chill-choked cough, and this—despite
the streets and streetlights, the city blocks aligned

with each other—is perhaps the only explanation
we can hope for: when the walls around us bend

like knees toward rapt radiators, their reflexes are
shocked as ours to find the earth moving again.

BELL

The man downstairs begins singing
Springsteen at six, as the one upstairs
sings prayers until interrupted
by the one of us who has not yet
adopted a practice: the baby,
who experiments boldly with volume,
timbre, and timing before
she finds a note that suits her
and cradles it with a full tongue.

*

The length of a human baby's vocal cords is two to three millimeters. Babies vibrate them very hard—harder than an adult could without injuring herself—to produce a grating sound, designed like the roar of a lion to generate response.

To replicate this effect, you can purchase training videos for rock vocalists called *The Zen of Screaming* and *The Zen of Screaming 2*.

In an interview, the proprietor says, "A scream should never feel like it sounds. It should never feel angry," before recounting an anecdote in which she yells at a woman in a parking lot.

*

After much exploration, Alyse finds a pair of earplugs that allows her to sleep through the baby's crying: Skull Screws, which have a "tough look" intended for musicians to wear while playing.

Alyse wears them to bed. They claim a protection level of 30 decibels.

Baby's cry: 110 dB.
Rock concert: 110 dB.

A sensation level of 110 dB is rated by sound proofers as "deafening." 130 dB means "physical pain." But they have an interest in the matter.

*

The *bel* was proposed by Bell Telephone Laboratories as a unit for rating the efficiency of telephone transmissions, but the *decibel* (one-tenth of a bel) is the most commonly used variant.

Bell, of course, for Alexander Graham.

The decibel has never been adopted by the International System of Units as standard, although petitions to include it have been considered.

*

Decibel ratings of things in our apartment:

40 dB: conversation
50 dB: air conditioner
60 dB: hair dryer
60 dB: stereo on average volume
65 dB: alarm clock
75 dB: flushing toilet
80 dB: ringing telephone
80 dB: cocktail party

Decibel ratings of things not in our apartment:

10 dB: rustle of leaves
50 dB: washing machine
    (related: 80 dB: laundromat)
50 dB: open office space
90 dB: subway train
112 dB: stereo on high volume
120 dB: ambulance siren
140 dB: airplane taking off
150 dB: firecracker
166 dB: handgun

*

In the room with a chimney, we hear
songs in the night that begin like wailing
but rush into praise in the early morning,
when we imagine the mother returns.

We imagine her progress. We find a clip
called "What Is in My Attic?" and play
the squeals of squirrels and the sharp tugs
of birds on the hearth for comparison.

We decide: bats. The landlord installs
a one-way flap, and one by one the voices
soften, become more distinct as others
emerge outside, gasping: I have forgotten

my keys and now I'm outside in
a towel. But it isn't that. We have never
needed keys, nor locked the doors.

*

As a child, Bell realized that if he was playing a piano
in one room, a piano in an adjoining room would begin

playing the same chords. Of course, we know
"Mr. Watson, come here, I want you," and the question

of whether he or his partner made it to the patent office
first. Minute differences in their models are evident

in the six-page application (two pages of drawn models)
on file for "Improvement in Telegraphy."

*

I have guilt about my suspicion of this baby, since I, as a baby, was both jaundiced and colicky—a delight, I'm sure.

*

Once, I had a cold and my father mailed me a neti pot. The attached note said that he did not usually put much faith in Eastern medicine but thought I might like this, "since you're a communist."

*

Let's take a moment to imagine Bell and his bushy hair
trotting down the street toward the patent office, bursting in
the double glass doors, and thrusting the application into the hands
of the first available clerk, some befuddled young man

with wire-rimmed glasses and a keen interest in chemistry,
fresh from Ohio. Historical inaccuracy: I imagine all scientists
as my father. The clerk's wavy shoulder-length haircut
is one such anachronism you'll have to excuse.

*

You see how this problematizes things:

> My father/Madame Curie dies of radiation sickness.
> My father/Tycho Brahe experiences kidney failure after attending a
>   dinner party.
> My father/Watson & Crick discovers the structure of DNA.
> My father/Robert Bunsen blows out his right eye with cyanide.
> My father/Carl Sagan explains the universe.
> My father/Jane Goodall roams the rain forests.
> My father/Henry Ford says that if he could be reincarnated, he would
>   like it to be as Henry Ford.
> My father/Nikola Tesla tests alternating currents.

My father/Rachel Carson takes a job with the U.S. Bureau of
Fisheries.

My father/Galileo blinds himself by staring into the sun.

*

There's a song in the musical *Street Scene*, which Langston Hughes wrote the
libretto for, in which two nursemaids bring their charges to the scene of a
murder so they can compare the tabloid pictures to the actual building façade
where a man climbing down was shot by his lover's husband.

The nurses offer baby phrases, like "Drowse, tiny tot. It shows how they got
shot" before the second baby starts crying and they switch to "Shut up, you
lug!"

*

Alyse believes that the baby is too old to cry so much, and so frequently. She
thinks she can identify the baby's age based on the cry's volume, and proposes
one: eighteen months.

We begin a surveillance effort to observe its size, since it rarely leaves the
apartment.

One day, we witness the baby looking down upon us on the sidewalk as we
carry in groceries.

As soon as it spots us, the blinds flip shut.

Alyse notes that it is large, and can close the blinds—too old to cry so much.

*

Infant age, and its associated acoustic features, seems to be a more important determinant of adults' perception of emotion intensity than are such adult characteristics as gender or infant-care experience.

*

I only have dreams in short intervals
of half-awareness in the morning—
as in, when the baby has awoken me
ten minutes before the alarm clock.
In such a moment, I imagine this:

I drag a piano to Chicago using a piece of string,
and when I arrive, I find that the house
I am to deliver it to is already occupied
by a woman playing a piano, in the exact
place I wish to place mine.

*

The actual transmission of a sound through a wall varies greatly
depending on the sound's pitch.
A human's ability to hear a range of pitches decreases with age.

The system of sound rating designed in 1961 for building materials,
Sound Transmission Class, only tests for the ability of walls
and windows to muffle sounds above 125 dB.

For sounds below that threshold, materials with a lower rating
may actually be more effective. It's an algorithm,
so, for the layperson, not particularly useful.

*

Bell's father was a professor of elocution.

One might assume, therefore, that no sound was lost
in the initial transmission due to human error.

One might also assume that no relationship
can be derived from this relationship at all.

When the device reached the public, Edison's model
was initially more popular because it was louder.

I LIKE THE MUSCLES ON THAT ONE

A. takes us to the Phillies game to watch
the players slam balls toward the outfield.

The muscles are the active organs of locomotion,

endowed with the property of contractability.
A. hopes to be endowed with the ability

to pick up a friend of a friend in the sports bar
on the second level of the stadium,

so he wears the tightest shirt he owns.

In man or woman, a clean, strong, firm-fibered body
is as beautiful as the most beautiful face.

He allows us half an inning of pump and release,
of the foul balls and big-screened likenesses,

before we finish watching what remains
from the panoramic screens above the bar,

just over the head of our friend
and a series of impassive women.

According to an online quiz and the personality
I imagine for Walt Whitman,

he would not sit through the innings, either.
In fact, if Whitman played a sport, it would be
    70% basketball
    60% golf
    55% swimming

which I like because I once knew a point guard
from Walt Whitman High School,

which was not nearly so remarkable

as the way she slunk down the court
and plunked the ball in the hoop over and over.

Whitman expresses an interest
not in swimming, but in the swimmer:

his luscious romp through the salty bay,
the transparent flush over his veined skin

over his opaque muscle
through the green-shine.

Examine these limbs, says Whitman,
they are very cunning.

Stripped, they are formed of bundles,
chemicals, a deep red color.

Exquisite.

The ultimate fiber of animal life

is capable of being either excited
or controlled by the efforts of the will.

If Whitman were a woman,
according to the sports quiz for ladies,

he would be inclined toward
       hiking
       ballroom dancing
       gentle exercise to help you refocus (yoga, Pilates, Tai Chi)

None of his rapidly swinging woodmen,
the lusty wrestlers on the vacant lot.

Just enough to keep the flesh not flabby,
good-sized arms and legs,

breast muscle, a pliant backbone and neck
for the bending

forward and backward
of rowers in rowboats.

The universe is a procession
with measured and beautiful motion.

According to the quiz, I should play tennis.

CHATTER

After winter, quiet except for logs settling
in the fire, the men begin to pick their way

up the ice roads, now mud, now earth again.
Occasionally with money, but usually

with need—the next closest camp
at least two days' walk, although

that family claims the edge of the world.
Siduri has thought of a sign—something to carve

your name in—but settles for allowing travelers
to wedge coins between the planks of the ceiling,

a memento before their crossings.
Glinting, one man asks: How much

do you think is up there? Not enough
to get me to hell and back, she replies.

VISITOR

While Gilgamesh rests, Siduri sits
on the stoop, back pressed against the door frame,

and waits for signs of the ferryman
on the horizon. Her eyesight has never been sharp—

nothing to threaten an approaching visitor
until he's close enough to throw stones—

but she's fast with a deadbolt.
It's dangerous, her mother writes, to live

all alone like that. People will talk. And how,
Siduri thinks, would I ever hear them?

SNAP

Siduri wakes to the swift rap of thunder
across the horizon; outside against

the wall, she watches waves flicker,
flashbulb frames. When the rain begins

to drum against her, she turns to press
her face to timber, rests her hands cupped

against a seam as though shouldering
its weight with a prayer. Her nose against

the planks, brittle with salt—
as though it might splinter, her tongue.

BABYLONIAN COMMERCIAL
COMPANY INTERVIEW, EXCERPT

Interviewer: You're aware that it's likely
                You won't have any customers
                                For several months, at least.
Siduri: Yes.

I: Will you have any family members traveling with you?
S: A wine glass.

I: Pets?
S: My voice, when it isn't lost.

I: What will you do during that time?
S: Practice my penmanship.

I: Really.
S: Play strip poker with the horsemaids.
    Translate the complete works of Philip Glass using the collision of
    sea-objects.
           Build temples out of firewood and burn them down.

INTENDED AMERICAN DICTIONARY

HOPE

Whitman has script that stretches to the margins
and a passion for eyes. In his list of men,
the physical detail he adds most often
isn't height, weight, or endowment—
but eye color, a detail attainable
only through mutual observation.

*

Bill (big, black round eyes, coarse)
John Campbell, round light complex,
        lymphatic, good – looks
John (light complex – light gray eyes)

"Victory" (James Dalton (20) roundfaced, lymphatic
        }   lost front teetch
13   (Jack – (20) little drawing of his head

*

The original text of *Gray's Anatomy: Descriptive and Surgical* appeared in 1858, three years after the first edition of *Leaves of Grass*. It defines the brain as the portion of the cerebro-spinal axis contained in the cranial cavity, composed of the cerebrum, cerebellum, pons Varolii, and medulla oblongata. *The size of the brain appears to bear a general relation to the intellectual capacity of the individual.*

*

Expectation crowns/ this
        extravagant promise—
possibility

INHABITIVENESS

If you're reading about phrenology,
you'll find lots of photos of men
casually resting their hands
on the heads of other men,
which is a truly under-used
position in photography.

*

I must not fail to
saturate my poems with
things, substantial,
American scenes, climates,
names, places,
words, fo permanent facts
(include every important
river and mountain
animals
trees
crops, grains, vegetables,
flowers

*

We would sometimes run up hills
on Saturday mornings if Coach
thought we had been out the night
before. The preferred punishment

was Alligator Mound, a burial site
three miles up and down. When

I think of graves, I think of
the midwestern sun rising all at once

like a hot bath, my legs slick and
sponge, the exact point of dehydration
that aches for just enough water
to walk out of the desert, Coach

appearing just as we reached
the alligator's neck, pouring
little Dixie cups along the back
bumper of her hatchback.

PHILOPROGENITIVENESS

Sometimes original paper moleskins,
sometimes pages sliced down to ¼-inch stubs,
sometimes scraps of articles (scientific, linguistic)

pasted in the binding by hand.
Little boxes of film wrapped
neatly in rough brown string.

Whitman, I think,
would like this string.

*

I'm reading *Leaves of Grass*
when the river by my window, running fast

with recent rain, carries a baby past
on its back. Sprinting from the shallow

rocks to the wider gorge where he pulls under,
the boy's mother grabs his ankle. This is

not a dream. A sob climbs from her body
and spreads itself across the riverbank to dry.

*

You can have the roll photocopied with one button, but I copy scraps by hand
in their original proportion—an effort to feel the time to fill the page with
script, then return with each underline, double underline, and the meticu-
lous tiny hands drawn in the margins.

CONCENTRATIVENESS

As a general rule, Whitman veers metaphorical when describing the body.

Gray's Anatomy	"I Sing the Body Electric"
Muscles & Fasciae, Upper Extremity	*arm-sinews*
Appendages of the Eye	*eye-fringes*
Organs of Respiration	*circling rivers of breath*

*

Toward the end of a catalogue in "I Sing the Body Electric," he abandons all hope and begins listing features like "the thin red jellies within you and within me" and "the curious sympathy one feels when feeling with the hand the naked meat of the body."

It's hard to tell the difference between his *u* and *n* sometimes, so months look like mouths.

*

I leave my watch set
to Alaska time for months
although neither of us is there

because maybe in some reality
we are—still morning,
I've stumbled out
to spoon grounds
into the coffee pot, shifting
foot to foot on the cold morning
tile without bothering

the lights, eyes
still opening in flaps
like a turkey hefting itself
over the road
on little wings, everything pulling it

back despite its complete
corporeal investment—
that tension right before

the line of hands broke,
when everyone was holding you
and releasing you simultaneously.

The coffee starts to drip;
hands appear around my waist.

LOCALITY

I spend some time trying to learn whether anyone still practices phrenology
with any seriousness. One group is earnest, but more entertaining are those
in on the joke. One man has written a chart inspired by a teen magazine. He
calls his process D-I-Y Skullistry.

By his reading, I am reflective and withdrawn;
possessed of great willpower; generous to a fault;
obsessed with the symmetry of romantic partners.

*

Lorenzo and Orson Fowler had a diverse set of business
interests: lecturing, publishing, and head-examining.
The brothers analyzed faculties and displayed
casts of admirable heads in their New York office.
Whitman reviewed several books on the subject
and praised their "bumpology" practice; his own results
were so excellent (mostly six on a seven-point scale)
that he published the results at least four times.

*

I have a minor in psychology, which
largely means that I have a psych textbook
on one of my shelves. Primarily, social
psych—herd movements and impulses
toward others, training and chemicals.
It's a view that fits my belief in patterns.
When it was my turn to be subject,
I looked for them—what's the trick?

The concealed compatriot? How are
the questions varied to divert attention
from the real subject at hand?

COMPARISON

I email Alyse, who is writing on a farm decorated with piles of empty gin bottles.

*

Kate Partridge   8:30 PM
to Alyse

marginal importance:
i am using phrenology on myself.

can you feel your head and draw where the bumps are so i can tell if we're com-
patible?

*

Alyse Knorr   9:04 PM
to me

i really have NO IDEA how to do this. my head feels smooth.

*

Alyse Knorr   9:05 PM
to me

it's probably a sign of our lack of compatibility that i don't know how to find my
bumps and you do

*

Knickerbocker Magazine put out "Phrenology,
Made Easy" in 1838 to clarify the "much-abused
science." In theory, not so outlandish—that different
capacities inhabit different regions of the brain.
Underdevelopment and overdevelopment are possible, as
in other organs; just as a weak bicep on the left arm can
be strengthened through curls, an inclination
to murder can sort into a job as a butcher
or a businessman with proper instruction.

SECRETIVENESS

In chemistry: regeneration
enacted by the transfer
of chemical compounds—

death to life. In theology,
Paley's argument: the function of bodies
            evidence of a benevolent god

Lamarck: traits acquired in this
lifetime, transferred down

*

Whitman looks for the expansive
landscape of America

in the body—a vigorous democracy
in the arms of butchers, faith
in the resilience of the reflex.

Emerson says, "Its ample geography
dazzles the imagination, and it will
not wait long for metres."

Whitman doesn't wait
for meters, or even for accurate
anatomy—he charges on

with the three-foot Latinate words he has
and proclaims the adhesiveness
and amativeness of all:

athletic and luscious
and vigorous as he wished to be;
to be old and good and gray.

*

employer—employee
offender—offendee
server—served
lover—lovee
hater—hatee
suspecter—suspectee
receiver—receivee

EVENTUALITY

Like the other components of *Leaves of Grass*, Whitman revised his phrenological chart between editions. There is no evidence that this was done in response to any change in the features of his head.

*

Kosmos, noun masculine or
                    feminine,
          a person who scope
          of mind, or whose
          range in a particular
          science, includes all,
          the whole ^*known* *universe*

*

The Fowlers had quirks, profession aside.
They asked the audience to write their own epitaphs
during lectures as a source of inspiration.
Their program: rigorous self-reprimand
for unhealthful acts such as drinking coffee
or masturbation. Orson suggests, "STOP NOW
AND FOREVER, or abandon all hope."
Whitman, more tempered—he simply
reminds himself in journals
that his adhesiveness to Peter Doyle
is getting quite out of hand.

IDEALITY

You can imagine Whitman's delight
when Lorenzo Fowler told him,
"You are yourself at all times."
His head, "large and rounded
in every direction." This precisely met
the criteria for poets established
in the *American Phrenological Journal*.

*

Poetry, perfect-
                    ion, ecstasy, art—beloved
above the ho-hum

*

Kate Partridge   10:37 AM
to Alyse

I hate to be the one to tell you this, but your phrenological reading is rough.
According to these guys, you are a selfish, obscene murderess with little ability to
use hand tools.

All we have in common are our fear of death and extravagant hope.

*

        Such tests applied, we perceive
the astonishing spectacle of these
States, with the most heroic, copious,
and original supply of their own

native life= blood, life = motion, and
life – material, but yet, (with the
exception of cens[smudged] *and*
cheap newspapers – though those are
^{indeed^}*grand,) entirely without any physiog-*
nomy of their own.

*

However, be forewarned—people who marry someone "deficient" in the same aspects as yourself "will most sincerely regret that he had not paid more attention to the head, than to the face and feet, of his betrothed."

VITATIVENESS

Whitman referred to his work as situated
in the "laboratory of the mind"—as though
while his outside became progressively less
groomed, inside his skull little carpenters
and sailors were fiddling with a Bunsen burner,
concocting his new roughness.

*

Alyse responds by apologizing for her murderous temperament. She adds:
yesterday she was mad at someone, so she baked him brownies.

*

kosmical
(Prof. Olmstead says of the
aurora borealis "I con-
sider it kosmical in its
origin – not terrestrial.")

*

Whitman writes in *Democratic Vistas* of a "nation of supple and athletic
minds."

Meanwhile, the Fowlers proposed to *PHRENOLOGIZE OUR NATION,*
for thereby it will REFORM THE WORLD.

*

And I will make a new

song of riches, namely
the riches of the body

*

The walk back to the cabin—almost
as raucous as the bar, where men

and women in overalls downed
beers brewed next door.

A woman sings with a band,
boots, bandannas. Headlamps

pile with coats along sills.
Brimming. And the night, too—

cold in spurts plunging under
our scarves, snow blankets

lush by the roadside, pines
too sweet. Beyond the lilting bars

of the railroad tracks, the airfield
flicks its porch light

over a patch of road. Beyond,
the path slick enough,

dark enough—we should have
used the lamps. A soft cloud
of green on the tree line,
more pastel than starlight.

*

Even in advanced/ age, tenacity/ to life and rigor

M 4.0, 21 KM S OF KNIK-FAIRVIEW

Otherwise, a static day—
the snow huddled against the mountains,

the bike trail puddled over root-carved ravines,
we decided to go to war or not.

When I left, B. gave me a field guide
in a bar we frequented. I didn't read it

but went to a preserve to learn
to recognize my neighbors—

the bears fielding blueberries
from the paws of a young keeper

pitching them over the deck,
the caribou fencing, antlers clacking

like hockey sticks. In the gift shop,
a stack of pelts, fleshed and stretched;

a child stroking them and murmuring,
"Poor reindeer. Now he's dead."

A RANGE OF MANNERS, OR RATHER LACK OF

I wouldn't remember the path from the villa to the seaside road, except that
I'm sure it was beautiful, clodded with dirt, and while we were completing

our assigned summer sprints up and down it, shutting our eyes to the glow
     and grandeur
of the general effect, J. said: Are you running for yourself or to beat me? My
     answer,

then (young, leggy) was clearly the latter. But there was no one there to
     watch—the odd
passerby, I suppose, or the woman who prepared a meal each day for the
     travelers—

and who else is trained to have a moral microscope aimed at such antics?
The line between trained and training is not necessarily tense. What we can
     learn

from the train is its sense of purpose. I once rode a train to a remote
rain forest village where the same reproductions of Aboriginal art

were available, as everywhere else: in shop, street, theater, barroom, church.
On the return, the train stopped at the spot where officials held a picnic on
     the rails

upon the track's completion—wise, considering the advantages
enjoyed from that height: a sort of dry and flat Sahara rippling out

from beneath the lush ridges, a great moral and religious civilization
of trees. In the village was a zoo devoted to poisonous creatures—

painted, padded, dyed—with bad blood and the capacity for deceasing, a
     crowd

of petty grotesques behind glass plates. The officials held the picnic on the tracks
with formal table settings and a broad table carted up the mountain. I mean, in a cart.
And, in what I imagine as a pervading atmosphere of beautiful manners,

they took in the material luxuriance. Perhaps this is a shallow notion of beauty,
but I would like to be in the photo of old men in top hats, foppish.

Coming down to what is of the only real importance: what did they see below?
Athletes? Crops of youths, prematurely ripe? Art, perfect women, a rich people?

And the ones seated to face the mountain—shafts boarded over,
water trailing between cracks, rocks of muddy complexion?

I haven't said that there was any purpose to my trip except to see
what the people have done, which is always the goal in some way or another.

On the train, I had the seat next to the mountain. Before, everyone said, you will
find Australia to be much like America, which does seem to be the impulse.

#14 VISITS THE GALLERY

From its center, a bowl hoists a mound
of sanded stones, their girth barely fenced

by the carved perimeter. Not far below, a pedestal
dwindles. It's unclear which feat is the priority,

but I suppose we aren't being asked
to choose. Last week, I watched a bug race

around the metal rim of the porch table,
her brown a pleasant complement

to the forest green. She stopped halfway
between me and the wall, as though

maintaining the symmetry of the situation
might spare her. It did—not the symmetry

but her Viking antennae, her portly waist,
the inscriptions on her sides. She was someone's,

or her own. By the heaping bowl, I
encounter my friend Miller, whose first name

I don't remember in the moment, and,
anyway, she starts by introducing me

to her friend by my last name. We shake
hands, careful to meet without crossing

the low barrier for the alarm. In the courtyard
below, a circle of animal heads stares outward.

In a time when we barely knew how to touch
women's bodies, we went to a dark field

and knocked each other to the ground.
It is not that I am interested in women.

It is that I cannot figure out how
to throw myself completely into one.

COCTEAU

In Siduri's time, storms
pass like motorcycles

up the coast—blunt
and roaring in their paths,

but brief. She improvises
a shelter—her back below

the thick spine of the table,
the only restraint against

walking into the wind,
pitchy outside between

bursts of sand, static song
she could disappear in

if not for the throbbing
in her teeth.

COLLECTION

In spring, the bears emerge and fill
their recessed bellies with fish.
Anxious, the stream of mourners stands
in the tide, collecting seaweed around
their ankles. Come inside, she says, wait
for the ferryman. Siduri nets them
with another round poured in fresh cups
along the table. By fall, the bears
are bloated, harmless as old drunks.

SHOCKING, IF YOU'VE SEEN THE DAVID ATTENBOROUGH DOCUMENTARY

Siduri learned early on, after a surprising refraction during a game of wallball, that the horsemaids liked playing handball too—although, in their case, the long flanks of their tails made better receiving arms than their hooves.

On the loneliest nights, this is what she misses: quads burning like hot sand, the weight of the ball against her palm like a lover, waves of footsteps rushing around her feet: frozen moment in which she is the center, with half a second for muscles to decide which move comes next.

RESURRECTION BAY

In trees hemming the park from the water, eagles volley
cry after cry across plate glass pavement. Past a basketball

frozen in the net, icicles lace pickups to the ground,
and ravens line little shops with murals. In the coffee house,

I nestle with books in a chair by the vaulted window, pocked
by a hole the size of a tangerine, or a beak, I suppose,

the remaining pane cracked in joints as though strangely grafted.
The heat rambles out in wisps, like the hikers tracing

the ridge just prodding through deep fog. In an hour,
the eagles have met in one tree, still squalling at the bay.

UPON SEEING HER

She describes her first experience
    of grief: a fish jumps from its bowl
        upon seeing her. Or upon seeing her,
        a fish was so taken by the universe that

it could no longer wait to see more.
    Translation: Shostakovich makes me
        want to put things in my mouth. This could be Freud-
        ian, or a method of expressing myself

simply. I spend enough time fumbling
    with keys. One night the power goes out
        in the whole apartment except the bedroom,
        which I read as the universe saying, once more

with gusto, put me in your mouth. Or
    keep this apartment. We are here
        already, burying the fish in the pipes,
        burning candles, putting our mouths on each other.

CONCUSSION

In 1966, Ommaya et al. strapped
eighty rhesus monkeys into chairs

and administered blows to the head
with four-pound pistons, ranging from

a gentle tap to a fatal blow. The criteria
for concussion: abolition of response.

The greatest difficulty with such a model
is evaluation of consciousness

in animals. Results in which the skull
was fractured were thrown out.

*

Medical and Physical Journal (1803):

*The term conveys not
a precise idea of the derangement*

*produced in the organization
of the brain by external violence*

*

*also, -fuse: the part of a shell ignited by the aerial concussion of a preceding
bomb*

*

In college, I was paired with the strongest opponent
for one tackling practice and thought I might die

before running a play. Let us say I made it
twenty yards before the impact, which pushed me

back five. Let us say that when I fell I thought first
of breathing and not of her long, long arms.

*

Ann Lee believed shaking was
an act of purification, sin

being purged from the body.
She was described as a *virago*—

heroic but to a lesser degree
than men. The last Shaker

community describes its mission
in her words: *put our hands*

to work and hearts to God, wholly
consumed. Please feel free to write:

The Shaker Society, 707 Shaker Road
New Gloucester, ME 04260

*

After the accident, I consider the trajectory
described in the news articles: what does it mean
for the body to be thrown by such impact?
We left early to take the bus to games;

on the way home, compared bruises.
I try to remember this and not her hair.

*

I often wake to a presence—
a near-perfect image of someone

I know well sitting next to me,
writing poems on the nightstand.

*

Alyse and I merge our bookshelves,
uncovering all sorts of duplications

and three copies of *Diving into the Wreck*.
From the next book:

how can I reconcile this
uncontrollable light

all the sacred openings

*

Wilfred Owen suffered a concussion.
Later, he was hit by a shell blast and lay

semiconscious in a shell crater, empty
save the remains of a friend.

It seemed that out of the battle I escaped
Down some profound dull tunnel.

My friend
I knew you in this dark.

*

The Sydney Opera House employs bouncers
to catch dancers leaping from stage into the wings.

They tried using mattresses suspended
like wrestling mats, but these were not

as well suited for absorption as human bodies,
and too late to widen the stage walls now.

*

One night I woke on the bus to the
impact of a deer on the front bumper

and watched as its body spun into
the dark median. We did not stop.
On her phone, the driver said,
This has been a bad deer week.

We emerged two hours later
to find the flat front smeared

with blood and an antler bearing
straight out from a headlight.

*

Alyse is watching zombie movies,
so she sleeps with my field hockey stick

beside the bed. If I were not here,
would she keep it? What would she do

with the plastic mouth guards
locked in the shape of my teeth?

*

Pick one moment that shakes.
I was sitting in a pizza shop

watching her at the counter
and someone else leaned over to ask

how long I had been in love.

THE FALL

No one on the road in either direction,
Siduri slips out the back door with a handful of biscuits.

The gulls have found a scrap—a shell, really—
of salmon, mostly consumed by the horsemaids.

One gull tugs the carcass into his own feet, almost
toppling; another stalks, waiting for the fall

to snatch the fish himself. Siduri has considered
sharing her biscuits, but doesn't want a pattern

of dependence—she's haven for only a few
nights, as long as the grieving wander.

TAKING STOCK

When Utnapishtim arrives in the dark
with more firewood, Siduri is in her usual

position—crying, feet propped on another
chair beside the hearth. She doesn't apologize

anymore, just nods to the stack of coins
on the counter and gestures at the bottle of wine.

He shrugs and adjusts his mittens, the mouths
of two wolves hinged between his fingers

and thumbs; makes a quick estimate of the woodpile,
leaves with the axe propped behind the door.

Siduri thinks to ask what time it is,
but decides that winter is close enough.

BABYLONIAN COMMERCIAL
COMPANY INTERVIEW, EXCERPT

I: Are you mourning anyone?

S: Used to hop the fence
       behind the school and line up
       twenty hockey balls across the fifty-yard line,
       then drill them into the cage
       one by one.

                        In our neighborhood,
       this sound was gunfire. Cops
       surrounded the field and flipped
       their headlights on at once.

           Bright!   Young!

           Strong!   Muscular!

I: Are you mourning anyone?

S: She was always going out in the dark.

DRUNK AGAIN

One December, Siduri threw a bottle of wine at the wall,
just to see. She used the one at the far end of the bar—bare

but for a few tacked maps amended with ink, etchings of paths
past and predicted. Tables and benches culled into a central mass, she

gripped the bottle like a throwing knife—by its neck; a quick toss
above her head projected its rotations. Siduri hurled so hard

the ridge of her tricep pulsed between swamp muck and mountain;
the bottle made landfall in the ranges cupping an inlet below

Quivira, neck fractured and surging like a geyser, coins dropping
from the ceiling into the flush of glass and wine.

THREE TIMES ON THE TRAIL,
I LOOKED BACK FOR YOU

At the corner where the pines beam
with Christmas bulbs,
            it began snowing,

and the next turn, the sky went blue.
I had almost forgotten
            the darkness, how it smolders

with depth. Say weight. Say raven. It vanished
just as quickly—gray an incantation
            over the brush

and hillside, snow gray, lung gray, ice terse
across the rink, ice plating the inlet.
            Say it another way.

The water pooling thin lakes above
your collarbone, steam rising into
            the towels, soft

scrape of your skis laying track
            along the path behind me.

EARTHQUAKE PARK

Someone has taken care
that all the edges should be jagged:

fence posts cut in descending steps,
path split by a constantly shifting

line up to the edge where houses
shrugged off into the ocean, remaining

ground rippling across trees locked
upward. From a rock along the inlet,

she observes the planes landing,
crossing before Susitna and selecting

the international landing to the west
or the local airfield to the north.

If she can identify all of the objects
in the sky, she believes in order.

Beneath her, the rocks boast
cartoon faces and phone numbers,

the recovery of ancient method
almost reverent to the location.

Another woman scampering farther on
the ridge slides down the mud bank

into a stand of grass, a collapsed circle
outlasting the animal that formed it.

ELEGY

When the dog, at last, is satisfied, we descend
from the highest peak we've dared test our spikes

on, a moderate hill in the park where others in boots
have pressed a system for feet in the ice trails.

As a matter of consistency, we hike, pause
at the overlook for photos, and turn to view the entire

mountain bowl, the ice unfurled across the water.
The hang gliders jump again at the chalet; they dawdle

across the soccer fields, a beautiful inflation
settling at the tree line. The dog favors them.

The trouble is, the mountains aren't metaphors,
or the dog, or the ice. They are not windows or guides,

chutes to the next place we want. In coming to mourn,
we avoid it. We can only eliminate the trails

around us, one by one, for slick danger. All wrapped
together in hills, the lowland and slush are ours.

ACKNOWLEDGMENTS

My gratitude to the editors of these publications, in which the following poems have appeared:

Alaska Quarterly Review, "Three times on the trail, I looked back for you"
Arts & Letters, "Ends of the Earth"
Better, "Bell" and "I Like the Muscles on That One"
Blackbird, "Chatter," "Visitor," and "Drunk Again"
buntdistrict, "Upon Seeing Her"
Carolina Quarterly, "#14 Visits the Gallery"
Colorado Review, "M 4.0, 21 km S of Knik-Fairview," "Earthquake Park," "Model,"
    and "A Range of Manners, or Rather Lack of"
cream city review, "Babylonian Commercial Company Interview, Excerpt," and
    "Cocteau"
Green Mountains Review Online, "Elegy" and "Resurrection Bay"
Passages North, "Taking Stock"
Pleiades, "Hope"

"Intended American Dictionary" was published as a chapbook by MIEL Books in 2016.

The poems "M 4.0, 21 km S of Knik-Fairview," "Earthquake Park," and "Model" appeared in the anthology *Building Fires in the Snow: A Collection of Alaska LGBTQ Short Fiction and Poetry.* Thanks to Martha Amore and Lucian Childs.

For their kindness and generous readings, I am grateful to Heather Adams, Jennifer Atkinson, Aisha Barnes, Kara Candito, Olena Kalytiak Davis, Joy Fraser, Lynn Hallquist, R. J. Hooker, Michele Johnson Huffman, Sally Keith, Éireann Lorsung, M. Mack, Sarah Marcus-Donnelly, Siwar Masannat, Bill Miller, Susanna Mishler, Mel Nichols, Cristian Núñez, Michael Palmer, Eric Pankey, Jeremy Pataky, Ian Ramsey, Srikanth Reddy, Meg Ronan, Elizabeth Savage, Ron Spatz, David Stevenson, Adam Tavel, Susan Tichy, and Michael Joseph Walsh. For their continuing foundation, Neil, Julia, Sarah, and Jessie Partridge, and Jeb Cooke.

I owe a great deal to the support of my colleagues at George Mason University, the University of Alaska Anchorage, and Gazing Grain Press. Thank you to the Vermont Studio Center and the Kimmel Harding Nelson Center for the Arts for the time and space to compose many of these poems. Thanks to 49 Writers for the opportunity to think about them in community.

I am also deeply appreciative of the efforts of University of Alaska Press to develop and encourage this work. My thanks to Peggy Shumaker, Amy Simpson, Krista West, and James Englehardt for their commitment and guidance.

Of course, the greatest thanks is due to Alyse Knorr, whose brightness has entered these poems in every conceivable way.

NOTES

Poems in this collection include language and information collaged from the following sources:

The Epic of Gilgamesh, translated by Benjamin R. Foster. *Field Guide* by Robert Hass. "Hymn to God, My God, In My Sickness" by John Donne. "The Myth of Anian" by Robert Owens, in *Journal of the History of Ideas*. "Qvivirae regnv, cum alijs versus borea" by Gerard de Jode, Rare Maps Collection, Alaska Digital Archives. "How Do Lions Grab Attention? They Roar Like Babies" by Stephanie Pappas, in *LiveScience*. "Hey, listen, if you must scream, at least do it right" by John Carucci, Associated Press. NetWell Noise Control. "Alexander Graham Bell," Lemelson-MIT. "More About Bell," PBS.org. "What Is a Decibel," Compact Appliance. *Handbook for Acoustic Ecology*, edited by Barry Truax. *Street Scene* by Kurt Weill, Langston Hughes, and Elmer Rice. "Adult Perception of Emotion Intensity in Human Infant Cries: Effects of Infant Age and Cry Acoustics" by D. W. Leger, R. A. Thompson, J. A. Merritt, and J. J. Benz, in *Child Development*. "Understanding STC," Saint-Gobain. *Walt Whitman: Poetry and Prose*, edited by Justin Kaplan. The Feinberg-Whitman Collection, Library of Congress. *Walt Whitman's America: A Cultural Biography* by David Reynolds. "Phrenology, Made Easy," *Knickerbocker Magazine*. "Phrenological Whitman," by Nathaniel Mackey, in *Conjunctions*. "The Bald Facts about Those Love Bumps" by Craig Hamilton-Parker. *Gray's Anatomy: Descriptive and Surgical* by Henry Gray. "Walt Whitman: The Miracle," by Malcolm Cowley, in *The New Republic*. "Phrenology and the Fine Arts" by Charles Colbert. *Orphée, directed by Jean Cocteau*. "Whiplash Injury and Brain Damage: An Experimental Study" by Ayub K. Ommaya et al., in *JAMA*. "On Concussion of the Brain" by W. Simmons, in *The London Medical and Physical Journal*. "Concussion," *Oxford English Dictionary*. Sabbathday Lake Shaker Village. *Diving into the Wreck* by Adrienne Rich. "Strange Meeting" by Wilfred Owen.